Contents

Daily Lessons

/s/ 2	/oa/ 22
/a/ 3	/ie/ 23
/t/ 4	/ee/ and /or/ 24
/i/ 5	/z/ 25
/p/ 6	/w/ 26
/n/ 7	/ng/ 27
/c k/ 8	/v/ 28
/e/ 9	/oo/ and /oo/ 29
/h/ 10	/y/ 30
/r/ 11	/x/ 31
/m/ 12	/ch/ 32
/d/ 13	/sh/ and tricky word I 33
/g/ 14	/th/, /th/ and the 34
/o/ 15	/qu/ and he, she 35
/u/ 16	/ou/ and me, we 36
/l/ 17	/oi/ and be 37
/f/ 18	/ue/ and was 38
/b/ 19	/er/ and to, do 39
/ai/ 20	/ar/ and are, all 40
/j/ 21	

Further practice

Tricky words 1 :.. 41
Tricky words 2 42
Reading and writing activities.. 43
Letter sound and tricky word review... 48

S s

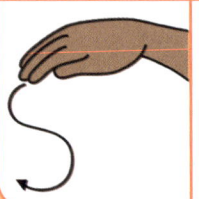

ACTION

Weave your hand in an ‹s› shape like a snake, and say *sssss*.

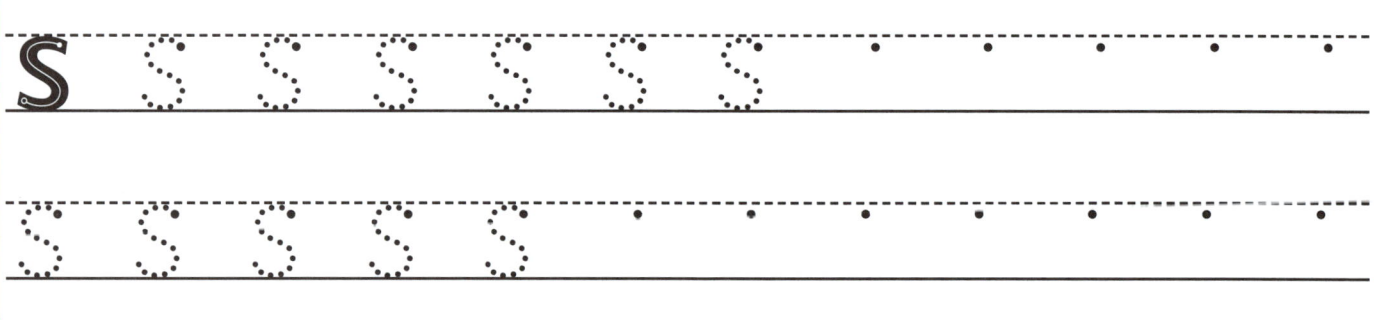

Say the word for each picture. Three have a /s/ sound at the beginning. Cross out the one that does not.

ACTION

Wiggle your fingers up your arm as if ants are crawling on you, and say *a, a, a, a!*

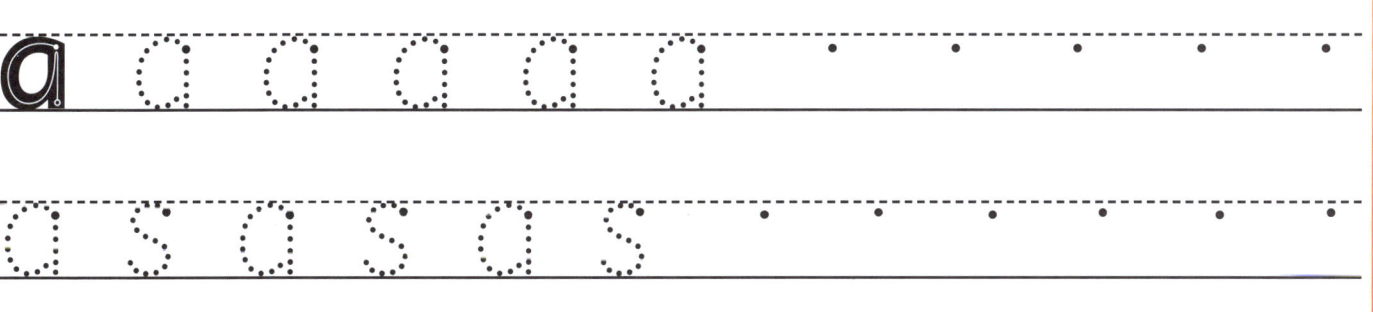

Say the word for each picture. Three have an /a/ sound at the beginning. Cross out the one that does not.

T t

ACTION

Turn your head from side to side as if you are watching tennis, and say *t, t, t, t.*

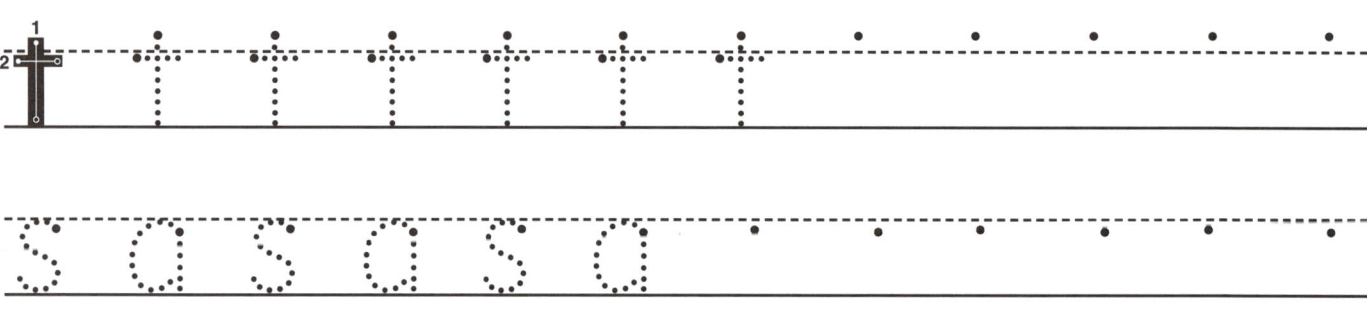

at

sat

Say the word for each picture. Three have a /t/ sound at the beginning. Cross out the one that does not.

I i

ACTION

Wiggle your fingers at the end of your nose as if you are a mouse stroking its whiskers, and squeak *i, i, i, i*.

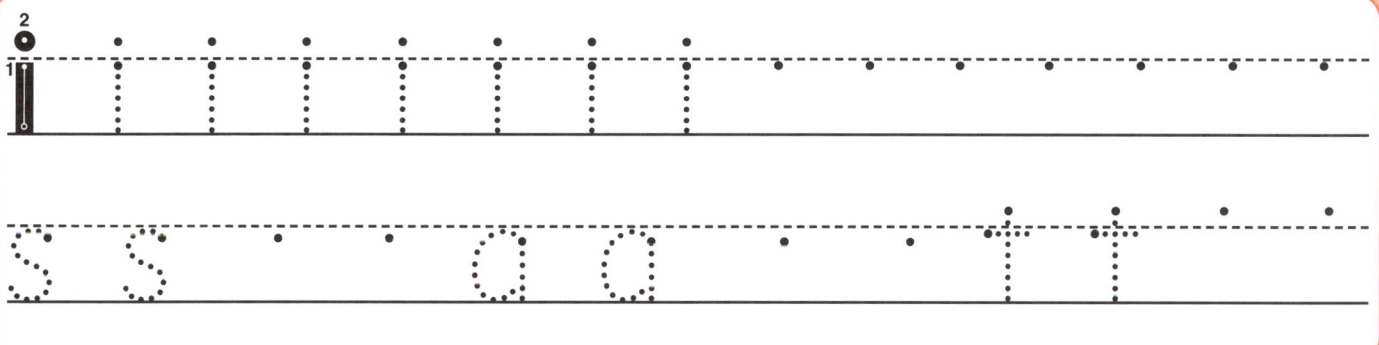

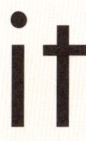
it

sit

Say the word for each picture. Three have an /i/ sound at the beginning. Cross out the one that does not.

P p

ACTION

Hold up your finger as if it is a candle and pretend to puff it out, saying *p, p, p, p*.

```
p p p p p p
s s a a t t i i
```

pit

pat

tip

tap

Say the word for each picture. Three have a /p/ sound at the beginning. Cross out the one that does not.

N n

ACTION

Pretend to be a plane with your arms out like wings, and say *nnnnnn*.

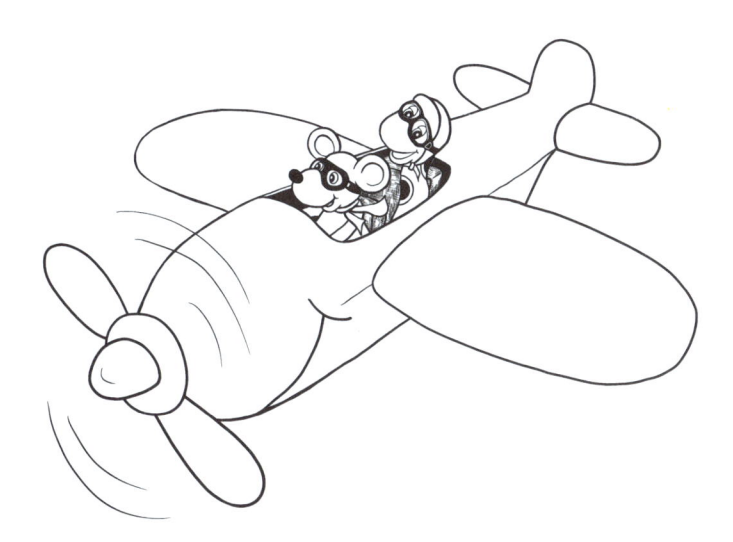

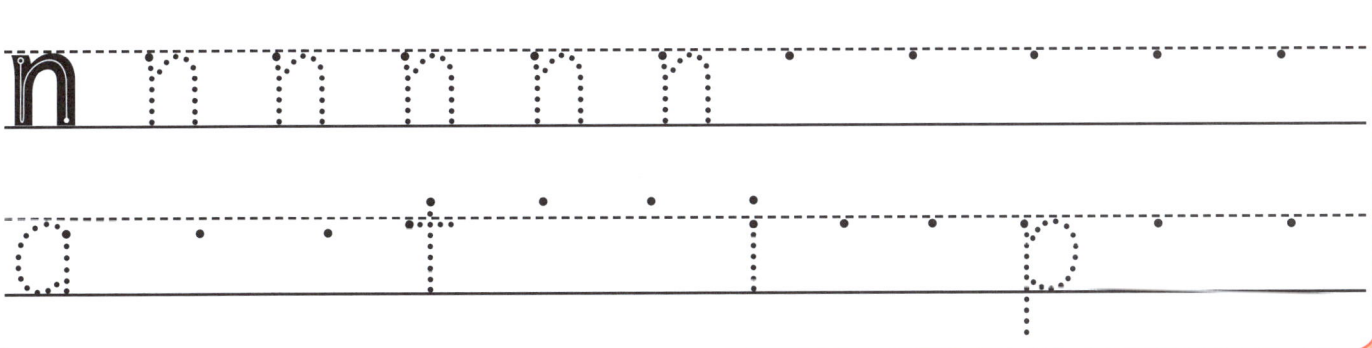

tin

ant

nip

pan

Say the word for each picture. Three have a /n/ sound at the beginning. Cross out the one that does not.

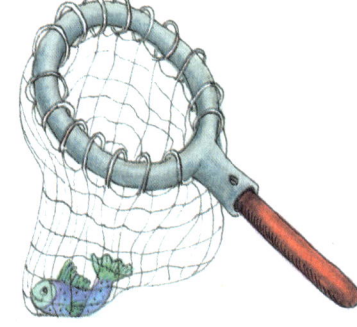

Cc Kk

ACTION

Snap your fingers together in the air as if you are playing castanets, and say *c, k, ck, ck*.

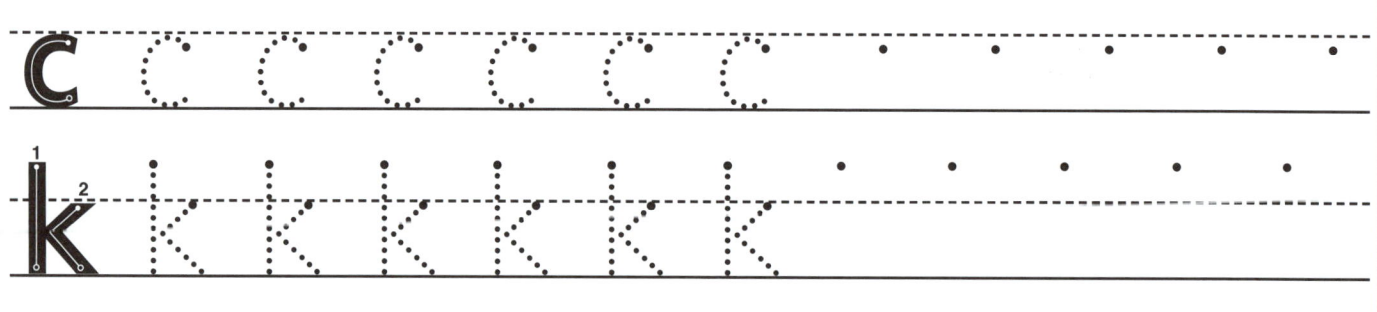

kit

cap

pick

sack

Say the word for each picture and write the letter for the first sound. Three start with caterpillar /c/ or kicking /k/, but one does not.

E e

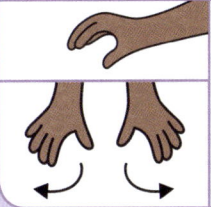

ACTION

Pretend to crack an egg against the side of a pan with one hand. Use both hands to open the shell, saying e, e, e, e.

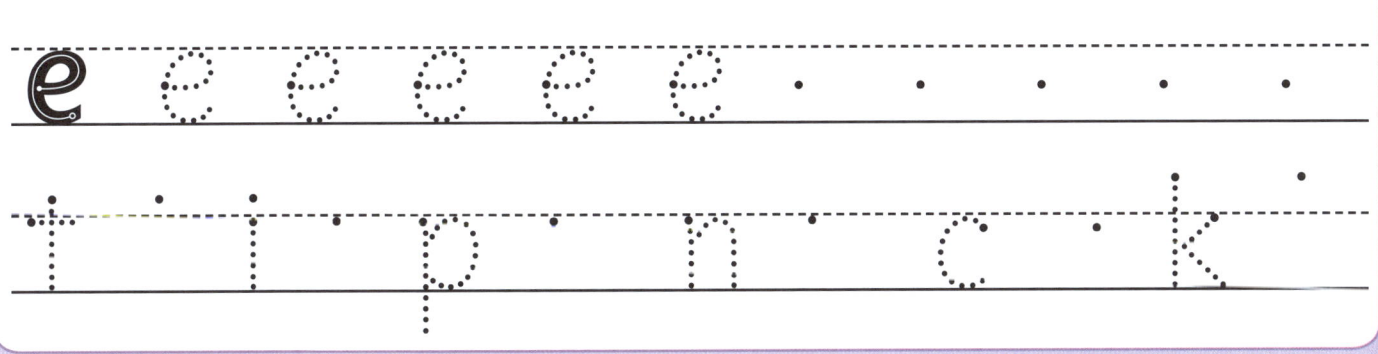

ten

pet

tent

neck

Say the word for each picture and write the letter for the first sound. Three start with /e/, but one does not.

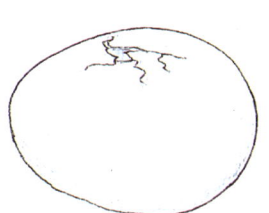

_____ _____

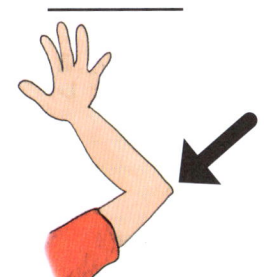

_____ _____

H h

ACTION

Hold your hand up to your mouth as if you are out of breath, and say *h, h, h, h.*

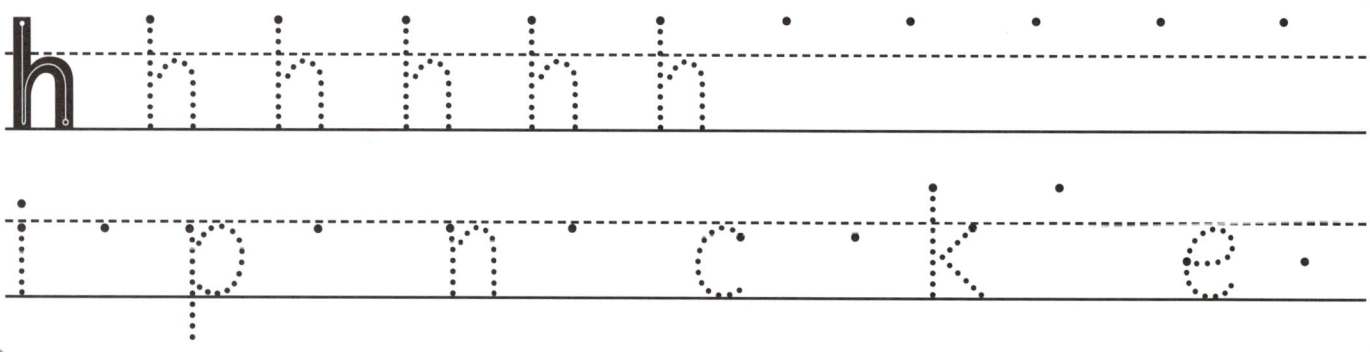

hip

hat

hen

hiss

Say the word for each picture and write the letter for the first sound. Three start with /h/, but one does not.

___ ___

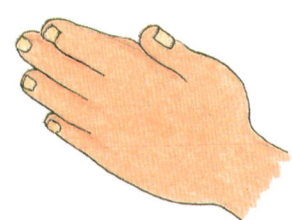

___ ___

R r

ACTION

Pretend to be a puppy pulling a rag and shake your head from side to side, saying *rrrrrr*.

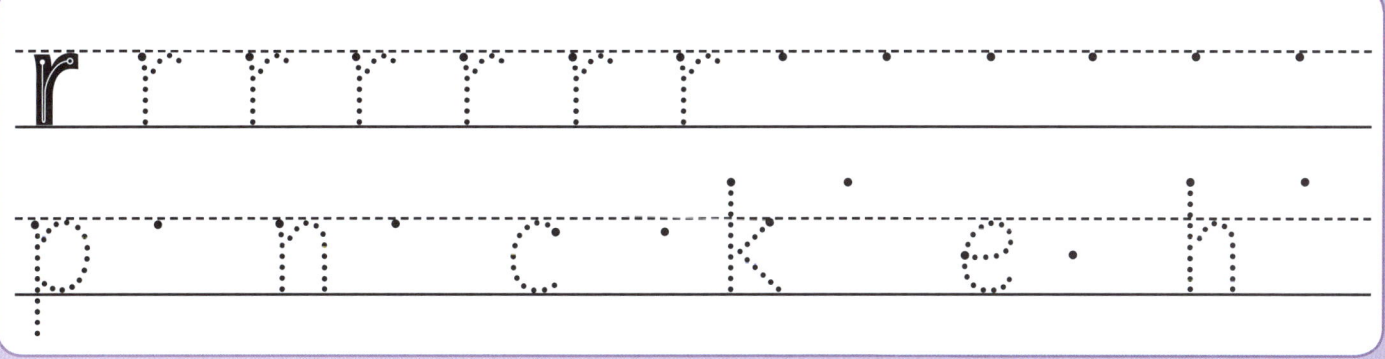

rip

rat

rest

trap

Say the word for each picture and write the letter for the first sound. Three start with /r/, but one does not.

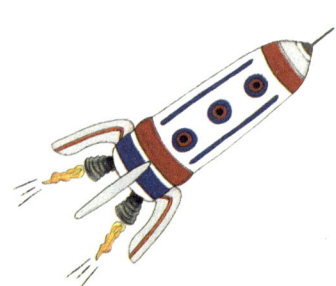

M m

ACTION

Rub your tummy as if you can see some tasty food, and say *mmmmmm*.

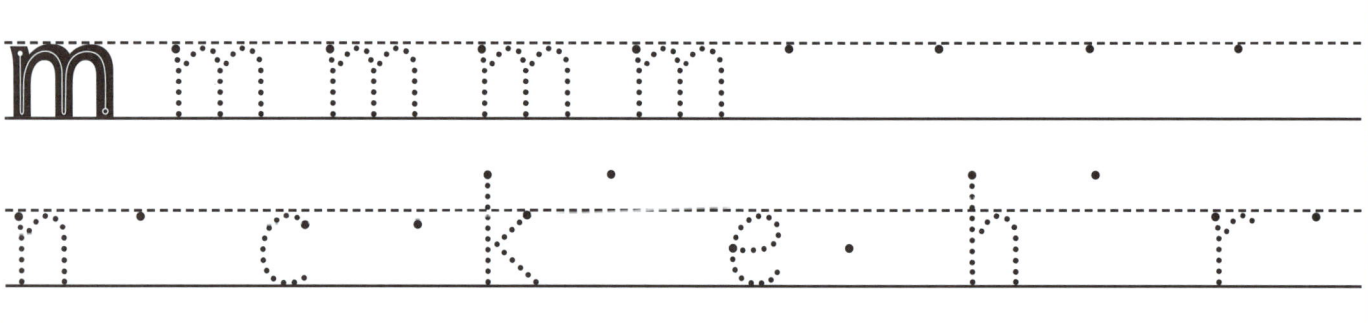

men

him

miss

man

Say the word for each picture and write the letter for the first sound. Three start with /m/, but one does not.

_____   _____

_____   _____

D d

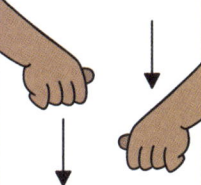

ACTION

Move your hands up and down as if you are beating a drum, and say d, d, d, d.

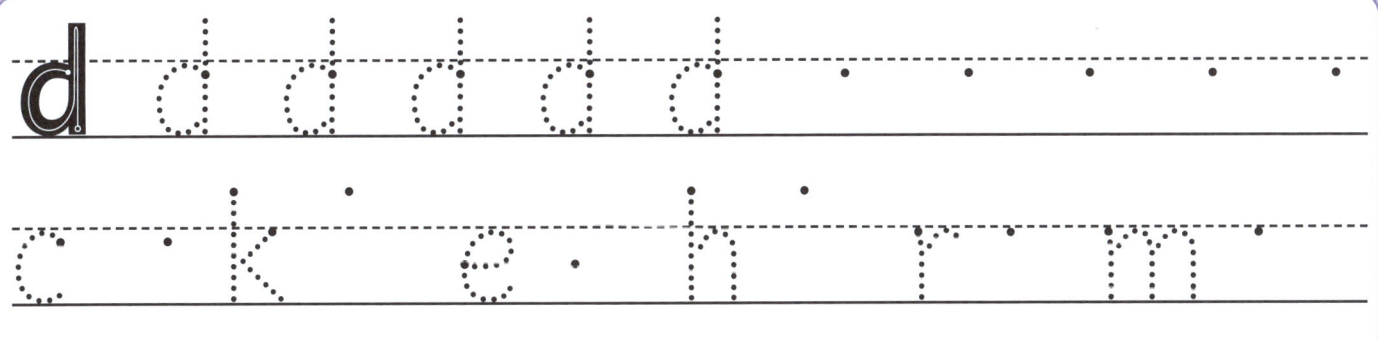

dip

red

dad

hand

Say the word for each picture and write the letter for the first sound. Three start with /d/, but one does not.

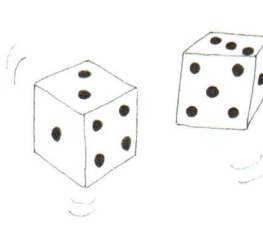

G g

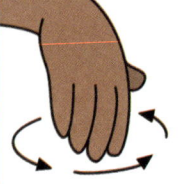

ACTION

Move your hand in a downward spiral like water gurgling down a drain, and say *g, g, g, g*.

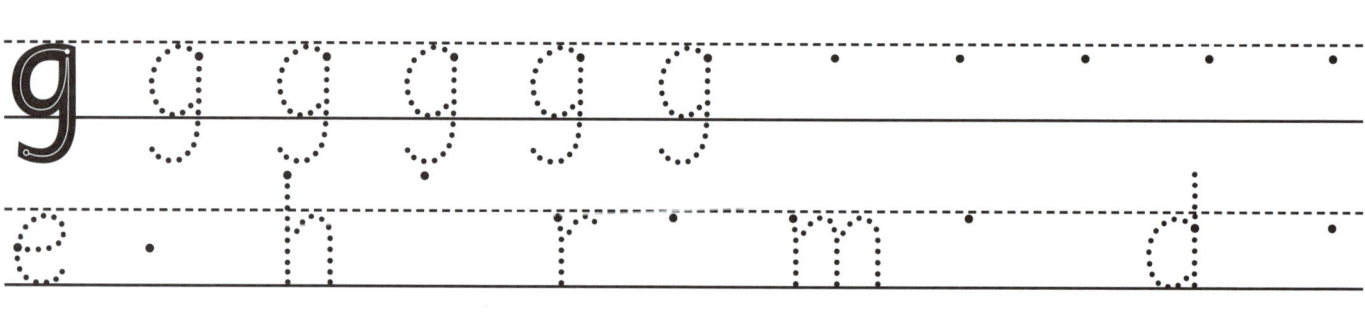

egg

dig

peg

grin

Say the word for each picture. Three have a /g/ sound in them. Cross out the one that does not.

ACTION

Pretend to turn a light switch on and off, and say *o-o, o-o*.

o o o o o o o

h r m d g

hot

dog

hop

socks

Say the word for each picture. Three have an /o/ sound in them. Cross out the one that does not.

U u

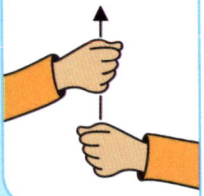

ACTION

Keep one hand steady and raise the other as if putting up an umbrella, and say *u, u, u, u*.

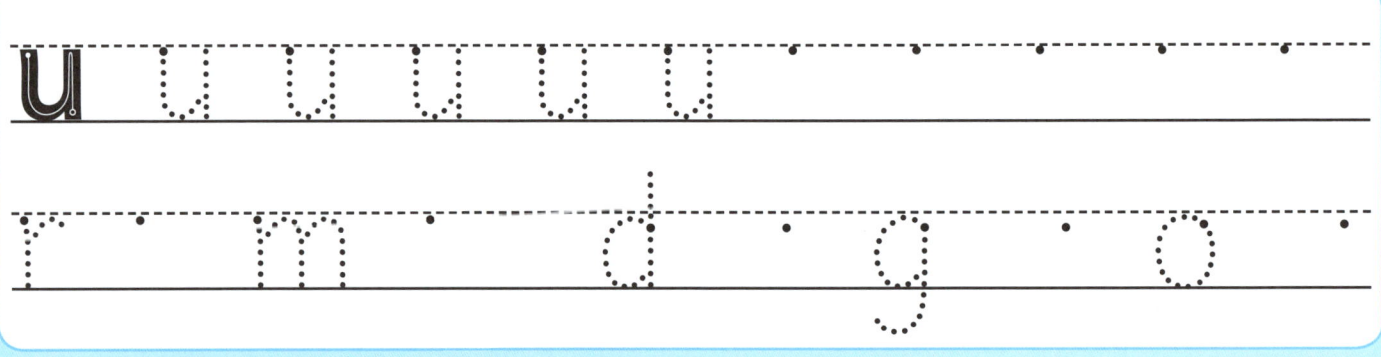

up

sun

mud

truck

Say the word for each picture. Three have an /u/ sound in them. Cross out the one that does not.

L l

ACTION

Pretend to lick a lollipop, saying /l/l/l/l/.

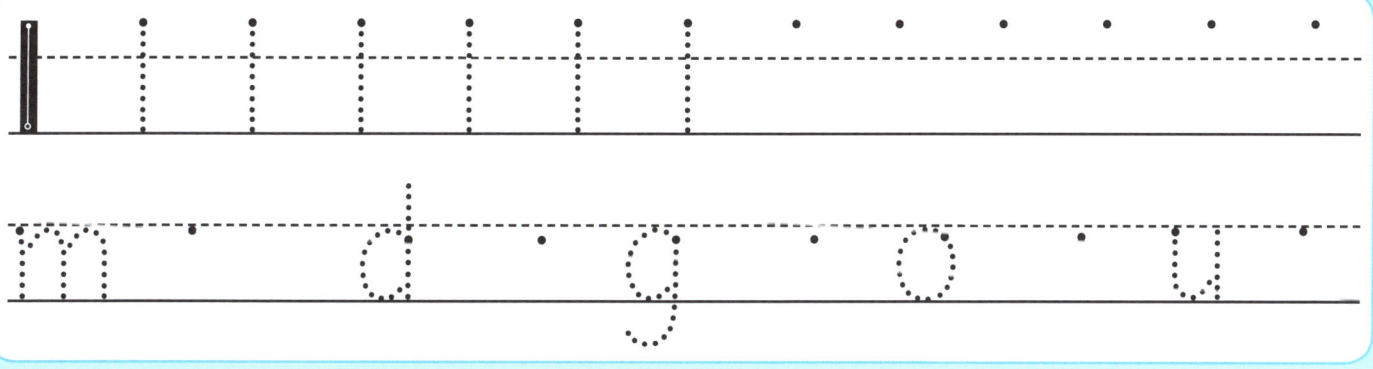

leg

lips

doll

help

Say the word for each picture. Three have a /l/ sound in them. Cross out the one that does not.

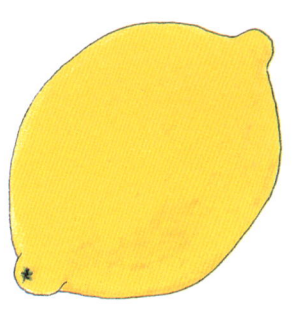

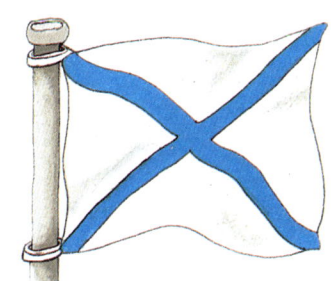

F f

ACTION

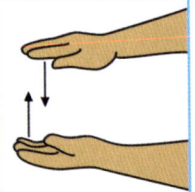

Slowly bring your hands together to mime an inflatable fish deflating, and say *fffff*.

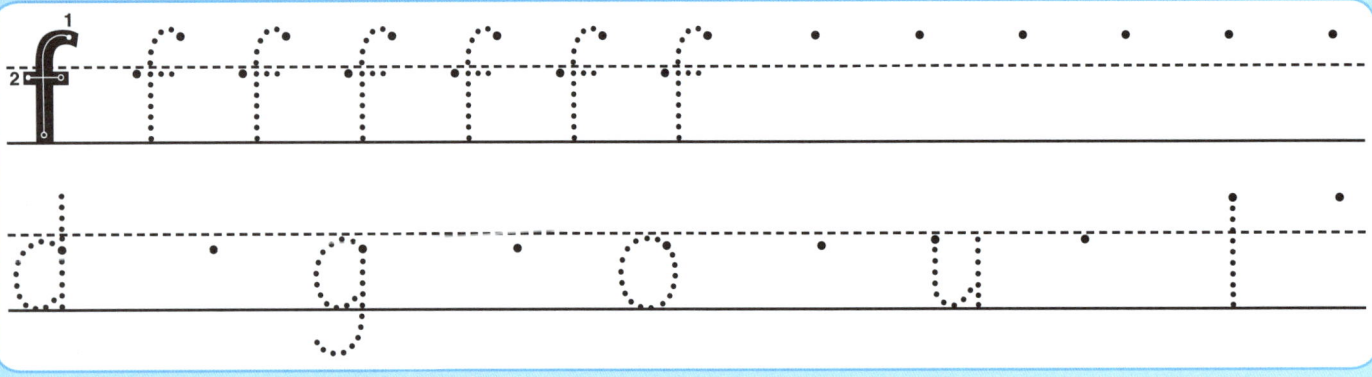

fit

fun

puff

soft

Say the word for each picture. Three have a /f/ sound in them. Cross out the one that does not.

B b

ACTION

Pretend to hit a ball with a bat, saying *b, b, b, b*.

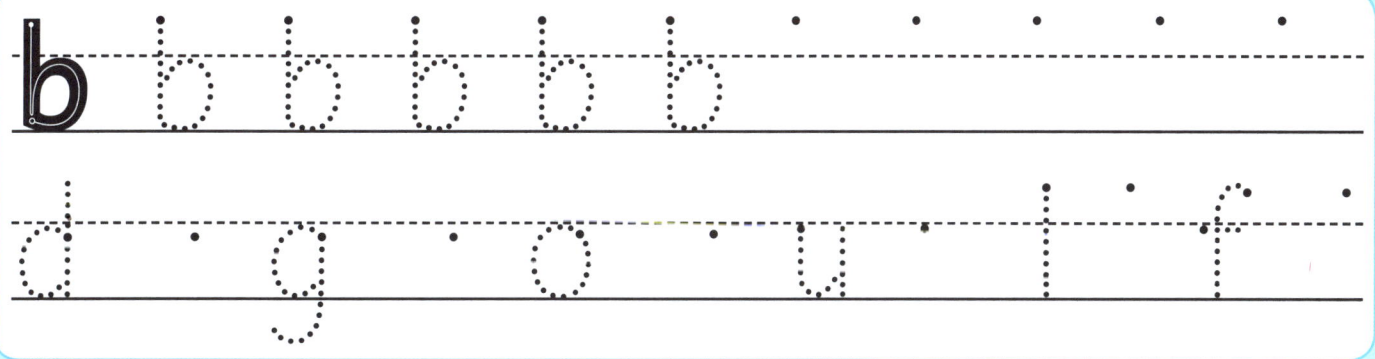

big

bag

bell

crab

Say the word for each picture. Three have a /b/ sound in them. Cross out the one that does not.

ai

ACTION

Cup your hand over your ear as if you are trying to hear something, and say *ai*?

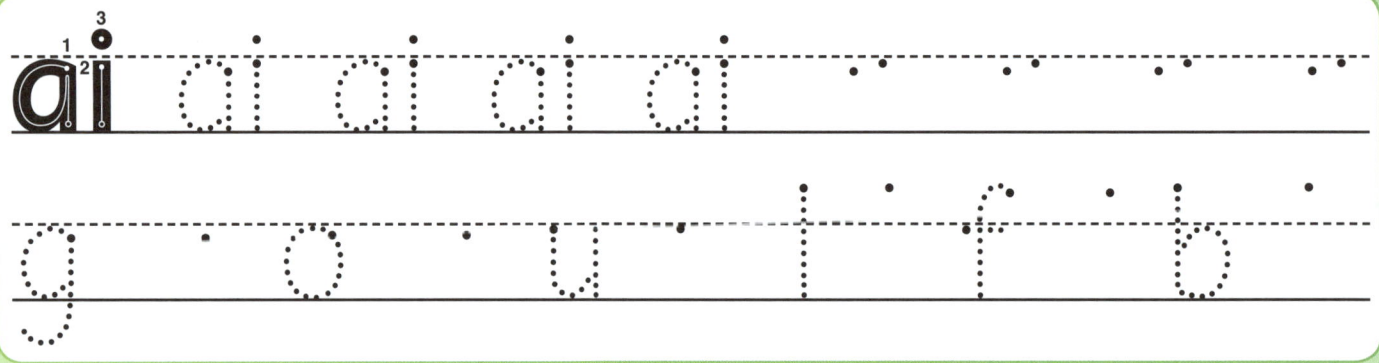

rain

tail

snail

paint

Look at each picture and say the sounds in the word. Write the letters for the /ai/ sound in the correct dot.

 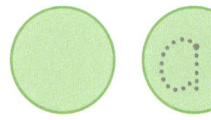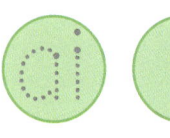

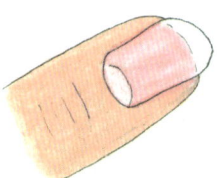 

J j

ACTION

Pretend to wobble like jello on a plate, saying j, j, j, j.

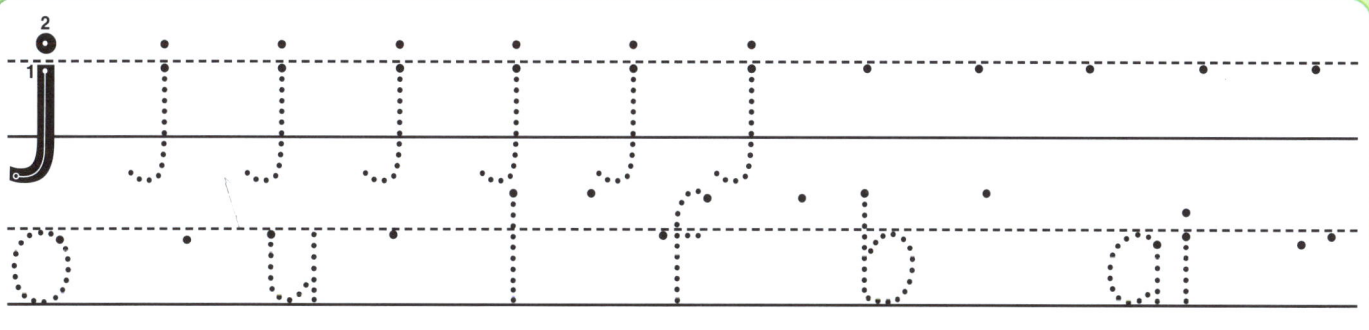

jet

jog

just

jump

Look at each picture and say the sounds in the word. Write the letter for the /j/ sound in the correct dot.

oa

ACTION

Bring your hand over your mouth as if something has gone wrong, and say *oa*!

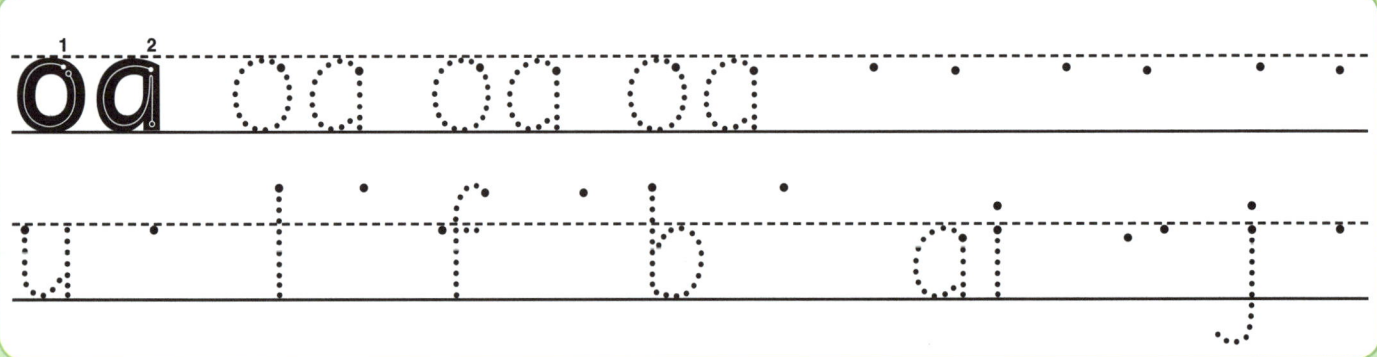

- goat
- road
- soap
- toast

Look at each picture and say the sounds in the word. Write the letters for the /oa/ sound in the correct dot.

ie

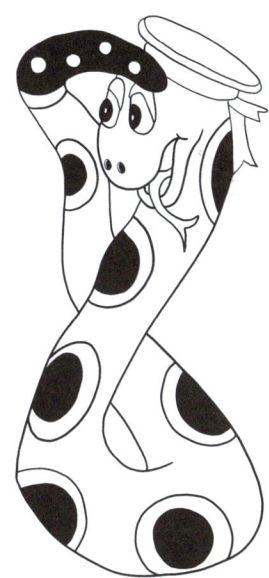

ACTION

Salute as if you are a sailor, saying *ie-ie*.

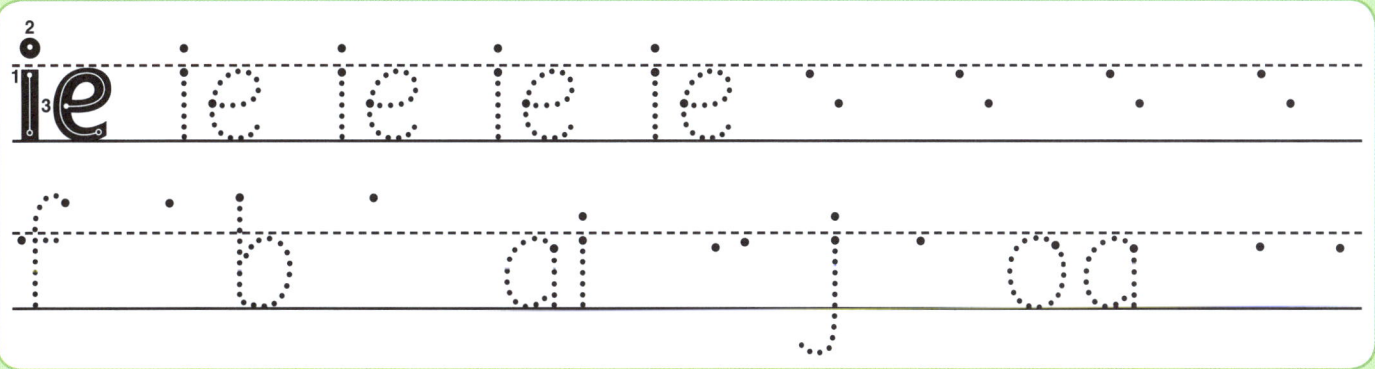

lie

tied

untie

magpie

Look at each picture and say the sounds in the word. Write the letters for the /ie/ sound in the correct dot.

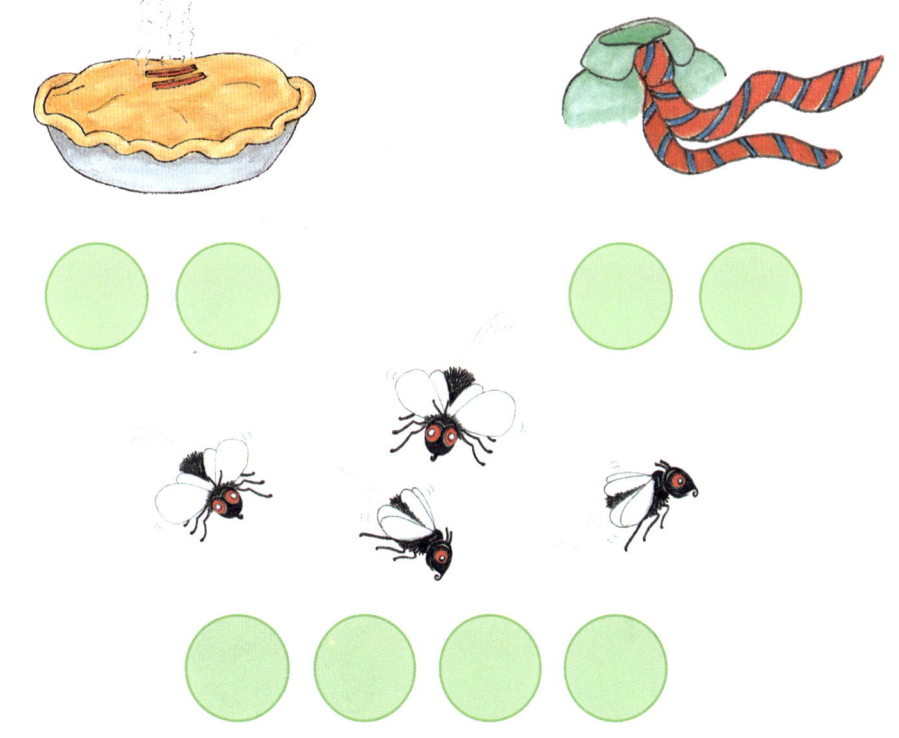

ee or

ACTION

Put your hands on your head like a donkey's ears. Point them up for *ee* and down for *or*.

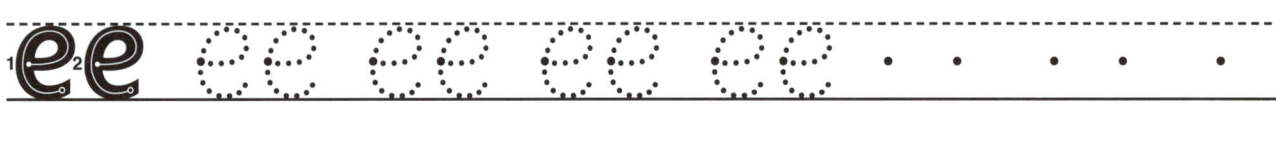
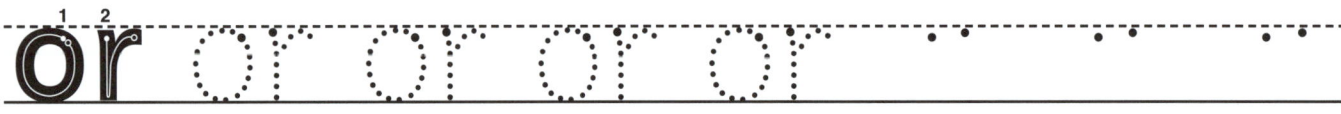

bee
tree
sleep

corn
fork
storm

Look at each picture and say the sounds in the word. Write the letters for the /ee/ or /or/ sound in the correct dot.

Z z

ACTION

Put your arms out at your sides and flap them like a bee, saying *zzzzzz*.

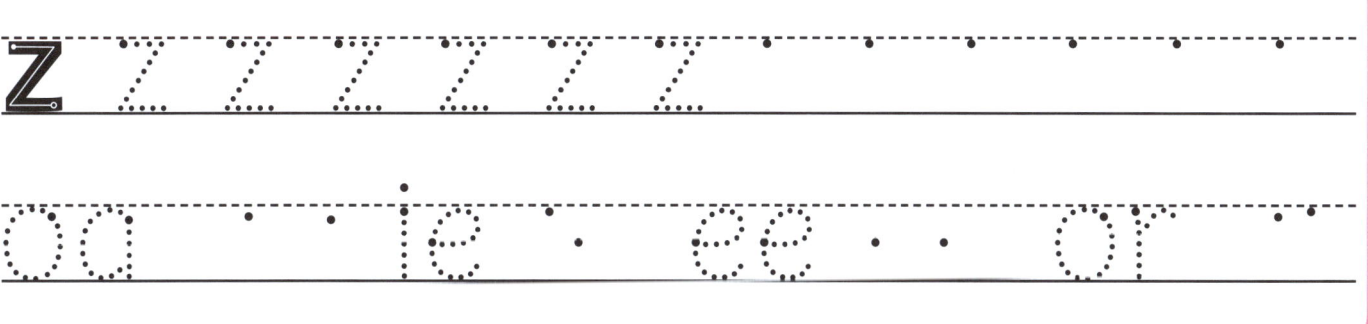

zap

buzz

fizz

unzip

Count the sounds in the word for each picture and color in the correct number of dots. Cross out the one that does not have a /z/ sound in it.

W w

ACTION

Blow onto your open hands as if you are the wind, saying *w, w, w, w*.

w w w w

ie   ee   or   z

web
twig
week
wind

Count the sounds in the word for each picture and color in the correct number of dots. Cross out the one that does not have a /w/ sound in it.

ng

ACTION
Pretend to be a weightlifter lifting a heavy weight above your head, and say *ng...*

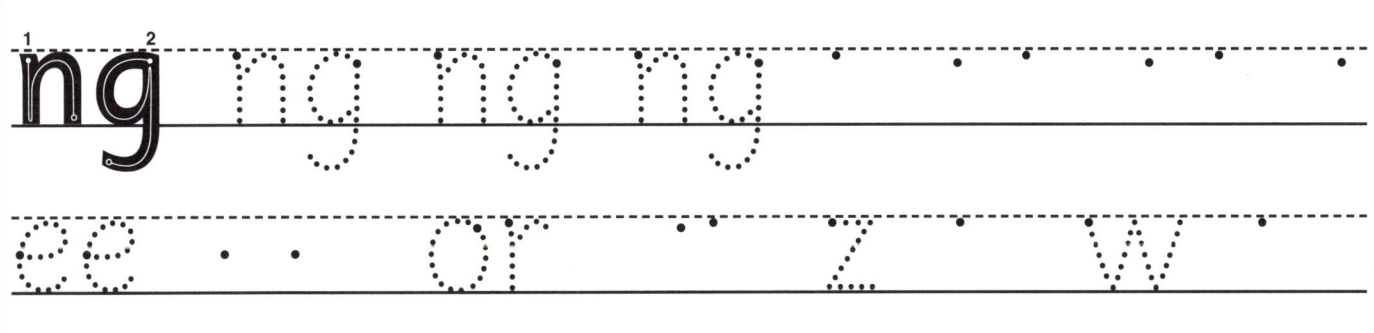

sing
· · ·

long
· · ·

bang
· · · ·

strong
· · · · ·

Count the sounds in the word for each picture and color in the correct number of dots. Cross out the one that does not have a /ng/ sound in it.

V v

ACTION

Pretend to be driving along in a van, saying *vvvvvv*.

v v v v v v v v

or z w ng

vet
· · ·

van
· · ·

vest
· · · ·

seven
· · · · ·

Count the sounds in the word for each picture and color in the correct number of dots. Cross out the one that does not have a /v/ sound in it.

○○○○○ ○○○○○

○○○○○ ○○○○○

oo oo

ACTION

Move your head back and forth like the cuckoo in a cuckoo clock, calling oo-oo, oo-oo (oo as in book, oo as in moon).

oo oo oo oo oo . . . . .

or z w ng v

foot
look
good

zoo
pool
moon

Count the sounds in the word for each picture and color in the correct number of dots. Cross out the ones that do not have an /oo/ or /oo/ sound in them.

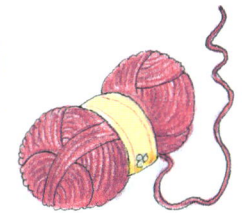

○○○○ ○○○○ ○○○○

○○○○ ○○○○ ○○○○

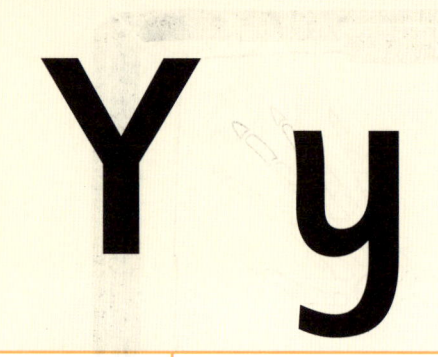

ACTION

Pretend to eat yogurt from a spoon, saying *y, y, y, y*.

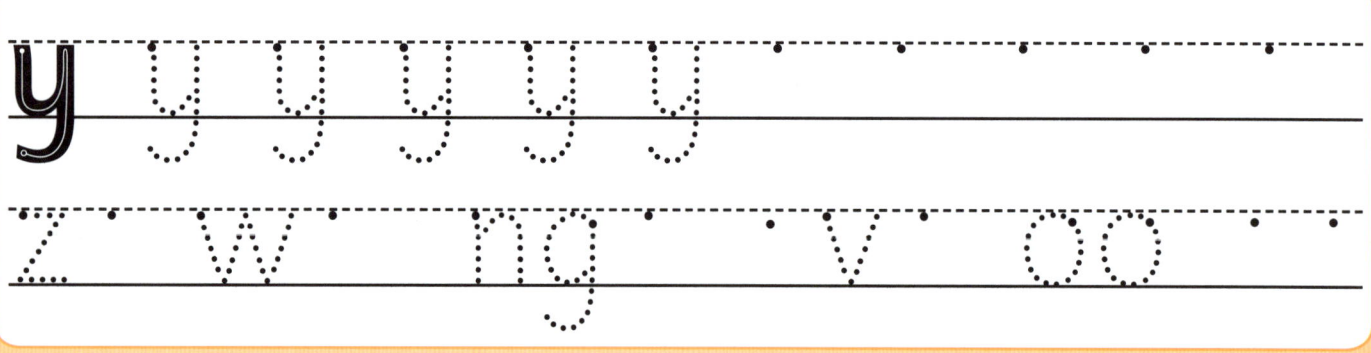

yes

yak

yell

yelp

Color in the correct number of sounds for each word. Write the letter for the /y/ sound in the correct dot.

X x

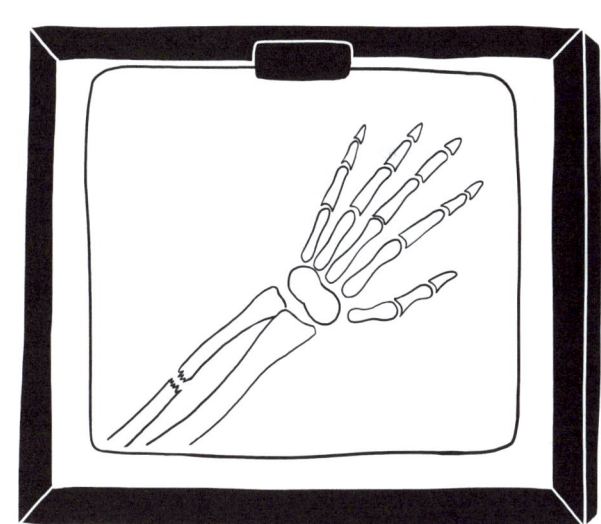

ACTION

Pretend to take an x-ray with an x-ray camera, saying *ks, ks, ks, ks*.

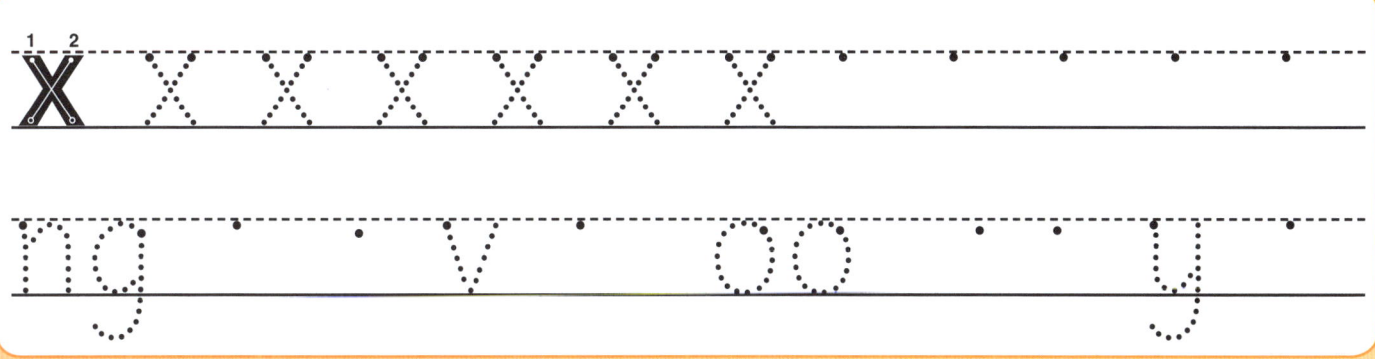

box
· · ·

mix
· · ·

exit
· · · ·

next
· · · ·

Color in the correct number of sounds for each word. Write the letter for the /x/ sound in the correct dot.

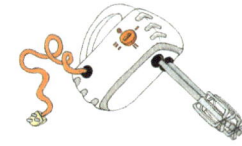 

ch

ACTION

Move your arms at your sides like a steam train, saying *ch, ch, ch, ch.*

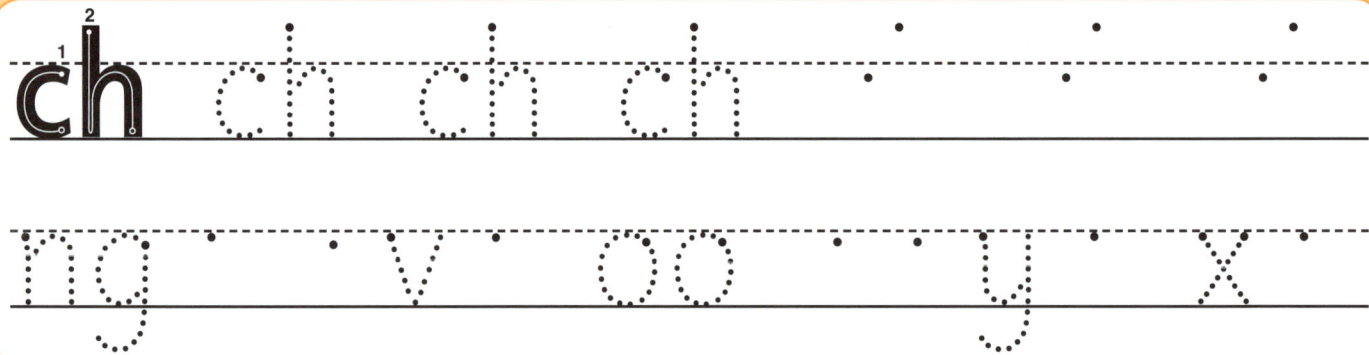

chop

chain

torch

bunch

Color in the correct number of sounds for each word. Write the letters for the /ch/ sound in the correct dot.

sh

ACTION

Place your index finger against your lips, and say *shshshsh*.

sh sh sh sh

v oo y x ch

dish

shop

sheep

brush

Color in the correct number of sounds for each word. Write the letters for the /sh/ sound in the correct dot.

33

th th

ACTION

Pretend to be a rude clown. Stick out your tongue a little for *th* (as in *this*) and further for *th* (as in *thumb*).

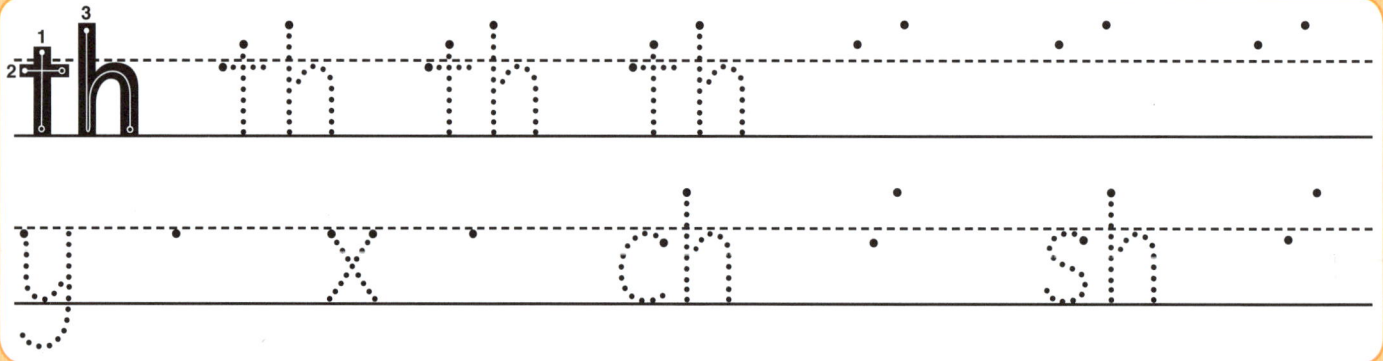

this
that
then

thin
moth
three

Color in the correct number of sounds for each word. Write the letters for the /th/ or /th/ sound in the correct dot.

Qu qu

he
she

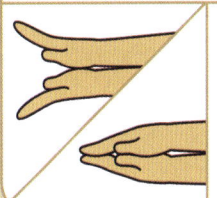

ACTION
Make a duck's beak with your hands and open and close it, saying *qu, qu, qu, qu*.

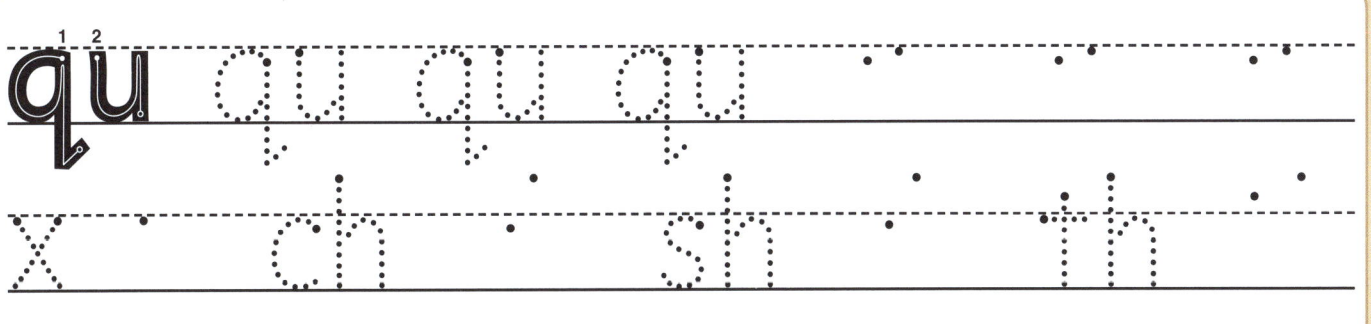

quiz

squid

quack

squirrel

Look at each picture and say the sounds in the word. Write the letters for the /qu/ sound in the correct dot.

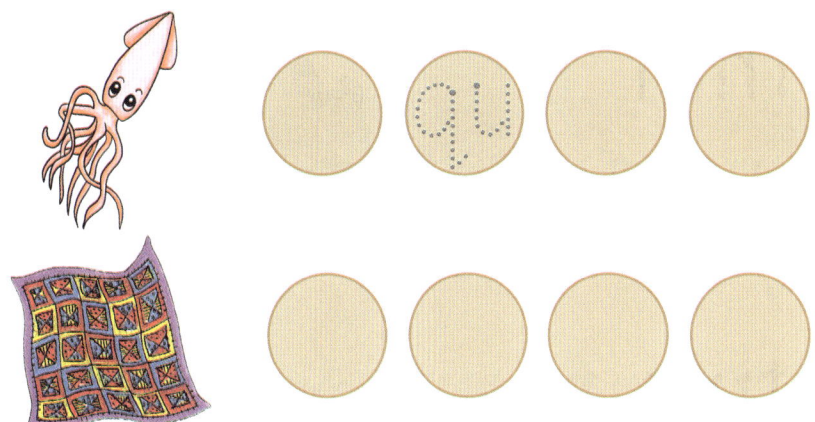

Write the word for the picture. Remember to listen for all the sounds in the word.

qu ee n

35

ou

me
we

ACTION
Pretend your finger is a needle and prick your thumb, saying *ou!*

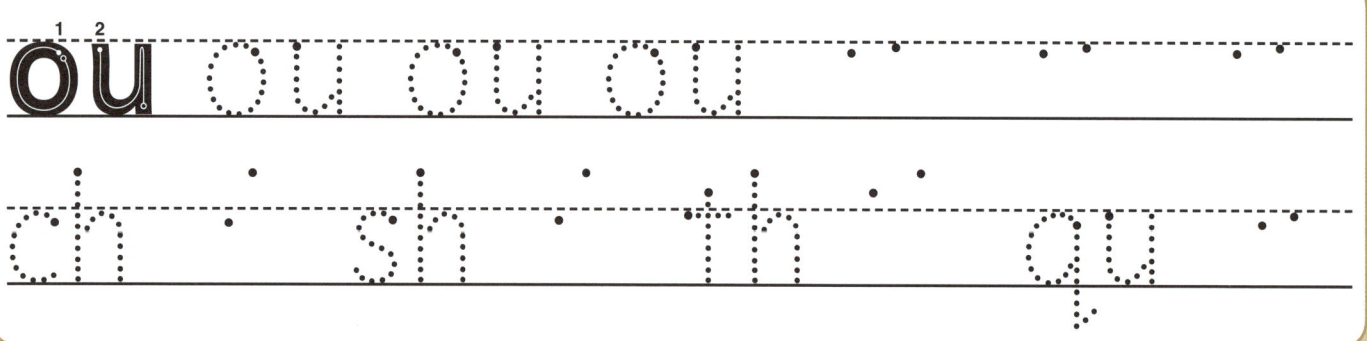

out
loud
shout
mouth

Look at each picture and say the sounds in the word. Write the letters for the /ou/ sound in the correct dot.

Write the word for the picture. Remember to listen for all the sounds in the word.

oi

ACTION

Cup your hands around your mouth as if you are hailing a passing boat, and say *oi, ship ahoy!*

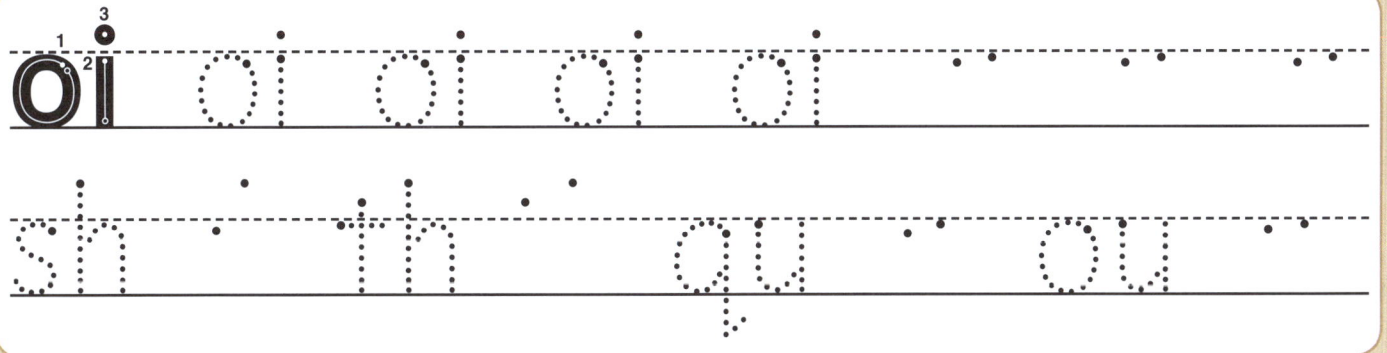

oil

join

soil

point

Look at each picture and say the sounds in the word. Write the letters for the /oi/ sound in the correct dot.

Write the word for the picture. Remember to listen for all the sounds in the word.

ue

ACTION

Point to people around you, and say *ue, ue, ue, ue*.

was

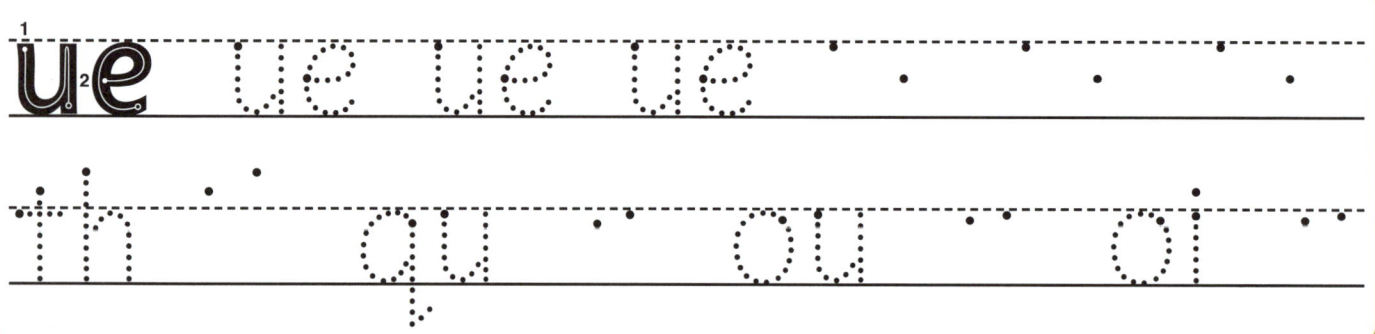

fuel

value

statue

continue

Look at each picture and say the sounds in the word. Write the letters for the /ue/ sound in the correct dot.

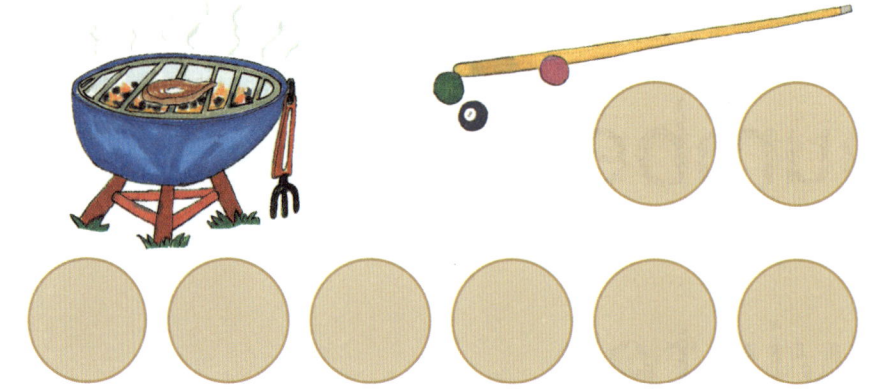

Write the word for the picture. Remember to listen for all the sounds in the word.

er

ACTION
Roll your hands over each other like a mixer, and say *er-er-er-er*.

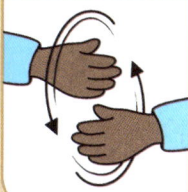

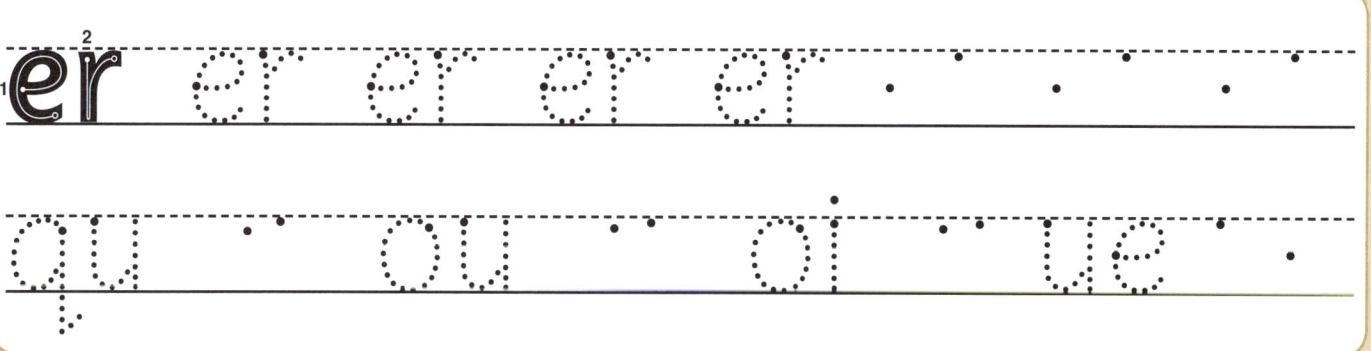

letter

number

winter

summer

Look at each picture and say the sounds in the word. Write the letters for the /er/ sound in the correct dot.

Write the word for the picture. Remember to listen for all the sounds in the word.

ar

are
all

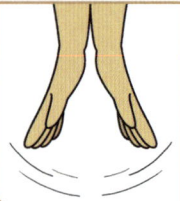

ACTION

Clap your hands loosely like a seal, and say *ar, ar, ar, ar*.

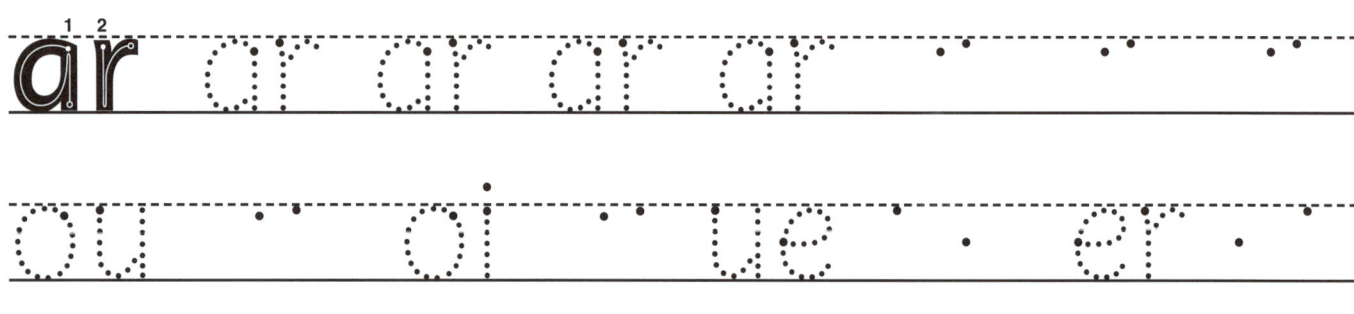

jar

dark

shark

farmer

Look at each picture and say the sounds in the word. Write the letters for the /ar/ sound in the correct dot.

Write the word for the picture. Remember to listen for all the sounds in the word.

Tricky Words 1

Read the words and underline the tricky bit.

Now try writing them. Say the word each time, listen for the sounds, and remember how to write the tricky bit.

Look Find the tricky bit.	Copy then Cover	Write then Check	Have another go!
the	the		
he	he		
she	she		
me	me		
we	we		
be	be		

41

Tricky Words 2

Read the words and underline the tricky bit.

Now try writing them. Say the word each time, listen for the sounds, and remember how to write the tricky bit.

Look Find the tricky bit.	Copy then Cover	Write then Check	Have another go!
I	I		
was	was		
to	to		
do	do		
are	are		
all	all		

Reading and Writing

1 Read the words and draw pictures to match.

ant · van · cup

2 Choose the right word and write it underneath the picture. Color the pictures in.

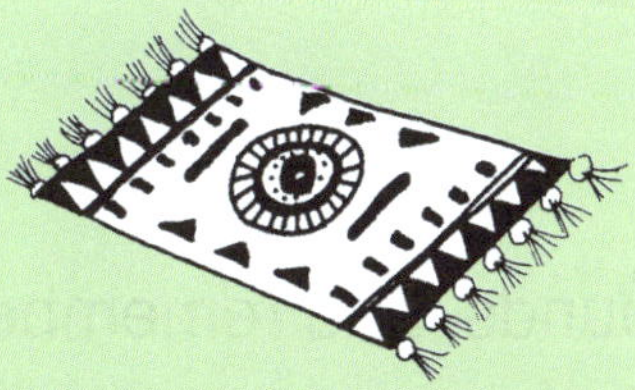

met mat man	log dig dog	sun run fun
m a t	_ _ _	_ _ _

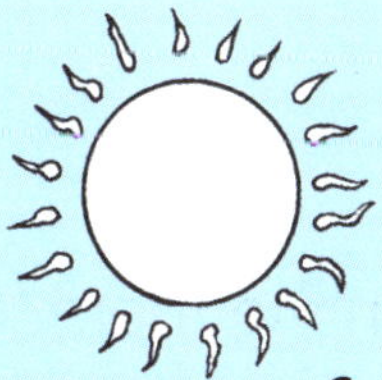

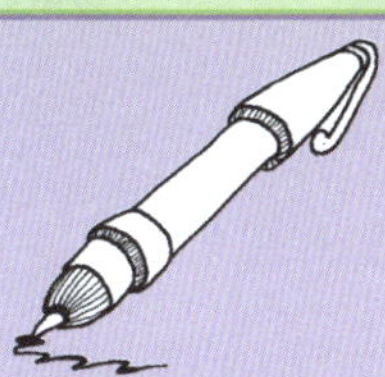

pet hen pen	net nut not	fix six fox
_ _ _	_ _ _	_ _ _

three trick tree	boot book boat	shark arm farm
_ _ _ _ _	_ _ _ _	_ _ _ _ _

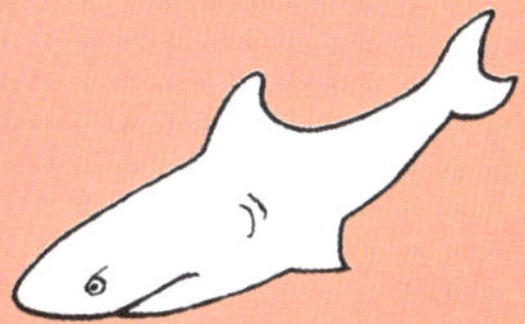

43

3 Read each word and match it to the right picture. Color the pictures in.

fork   dog   bus
mixer   statue
coin   bed   yak

4 Read these tricky words. Can you find them hidden below?

he, was, me, do, be, we, all, are, I, she, the, to

a	r	e	n	b	e
c	h	e	d	o	f
a	l	l	s	h	e
m	e	y	w	a	s
j	t	o	g	w	e
t	h	e	q	u	I

5 Read the sentences and draw a picture for each one.

This is me.

I can run.

6 Look at the pictures and write the words underneath.

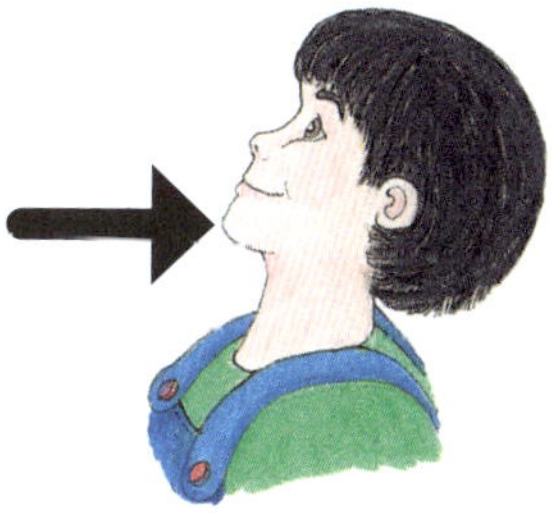

chin

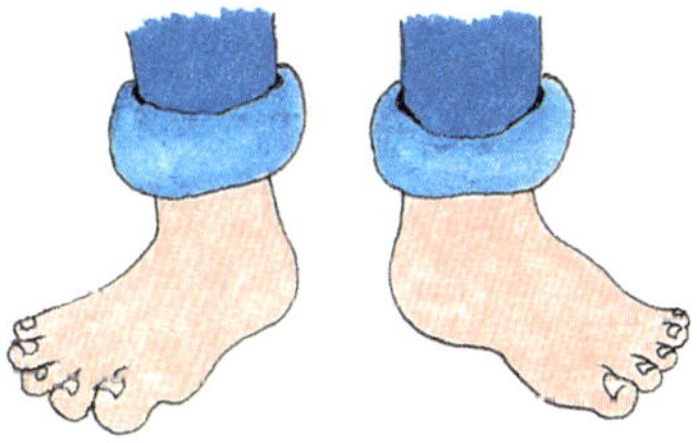

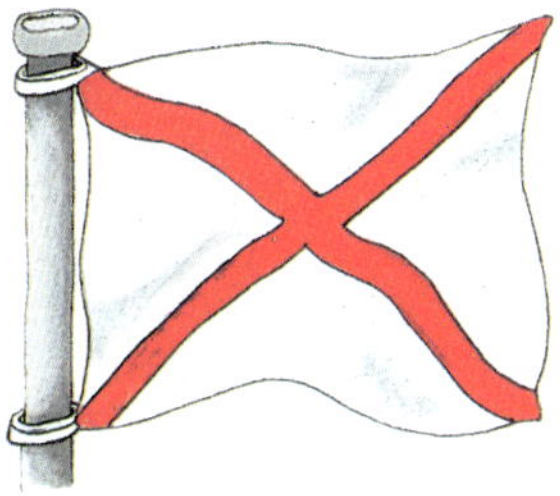

7 Read the sentences and draw a picture for each one.

8 Fill in the missing words to complete these sentences.

The ____ is hot.

The _____ croaks.

The _____ is big.

The ___ buzzes.

9 Fill in the missing words and color each picture to match the sentence.

The _____ is black.

I see the green _____.

We need pink _____.

The _____ is red.

47